BRAIN BLASTERS

AMAZING OBSERVATION PUZZLES

LISA REGAN

WINDMILL
BOOKS

CONTENTS

TIPS ON SOLVING PUZZLES FROM A WISE OLD BIRD

Here are some wise words to help you on your way.

Some of the puzzles are about finding a route. Use your finger to try different ones.

Certain puzzles require you to follow instructions. Work through each one, writing notes to help remember them.

Remember to read every puzzle carefully—one word can make all the difference.

If you get stuck on a puzzle, keep your cool and try reading it again carefully from the beginning.

ROCKET ROUTE

Find a route for the rocket to visit all the green planets, using only straight lines, and without crossing your own path or any red planets.

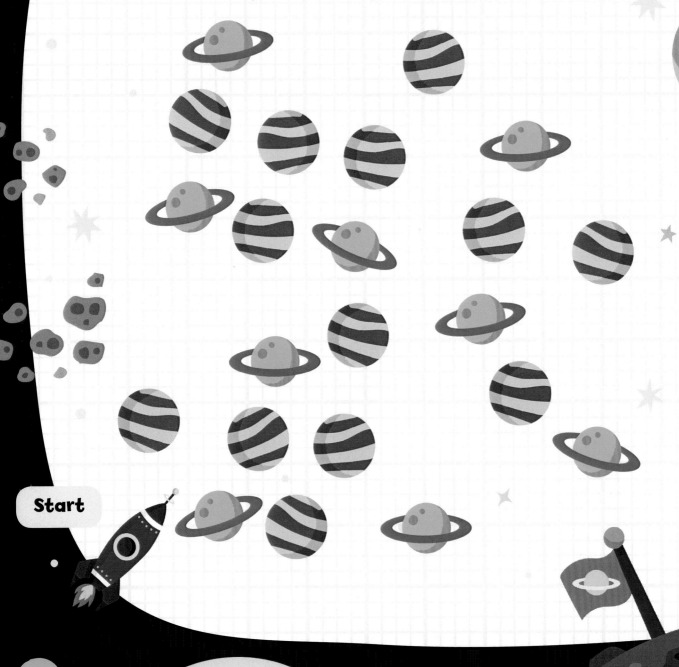

Start

Party Path

Each vehicle has its own start and directions to follow. Which one finds its way to the party, marked 📍?

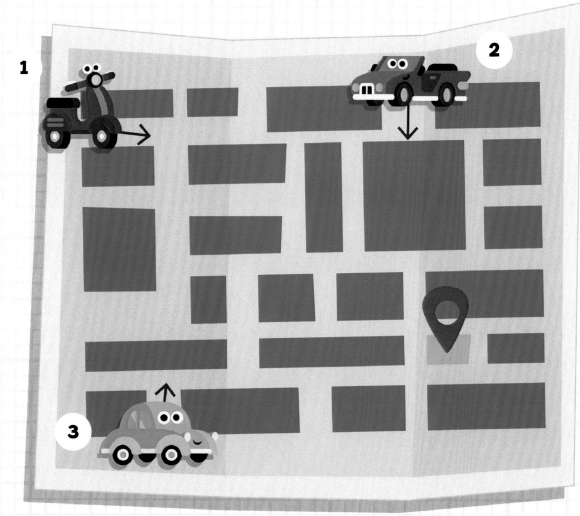

1

Take 1st right, 2nd left, 1st left, 1st right, 2nd right, 1st right, 2nd left, 1st right.

2

Take 1st right, 3rd left, 2nd right, 1st left, 1st left, 2nd right, 1st left, 2nd left.

3

Take 1st right, 1st left, 2nd left, 1st right, 1st left, 1st right, 4th right, 2nd left, 2nd right.

Hiker Trail

Find a route for the hiker from the start through all nine circles. Use four straight lines, and don't lift your finger off the page.

Start

Bike Track

Which instructions match the route taken by the cyclist? Where did she start from? The gap between each spot is one space.

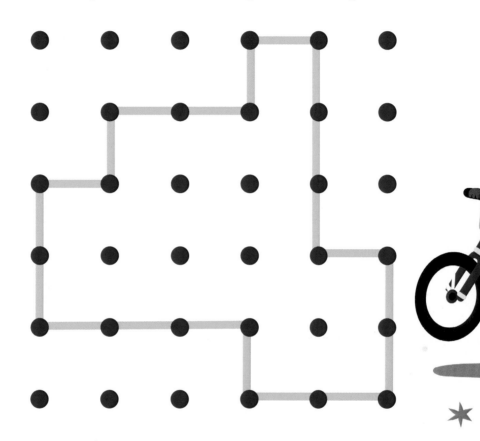

A

Go straight ahead 2 spaces. Turn right 1 space. Turn left 1 space. Turn right 2 spaces. Turn left 1 space. Turn right 1 space. Turn right 3 spaces. Turn left 1 space. Turn right 2 spaces. Turn right 2 spaces. Turn right 1 space. Turn left 1 space. You are now back at the start.

B

Go straight ahead 1 space. Turn right 3 spaces. Turn left 1 space. Turn left 1 space. Turn right 2 spaces. Turn left 1 space. Turn right 1 space. Turn left 2 spaces. Turn left 3 spaces. Turn right 1 space. Turn left 2 spaces. Turn left 2 spaces. You are now back at the start.

C

Go straight ahead 3 spaces. Turn left 1 space. Turn right 2 spaces. Turn right 2 spaces. Turn right 1 space. Turn left 3 spaces. Turn right 2 spaces. Turn right 1 space. Turn left 1 space. Turn right 1 space. Turn left 2 spaces. Turn right 2 spaces. You are now back at the start.

Robot Reboot

Which collection of parts is the correct set needed to build this robot?

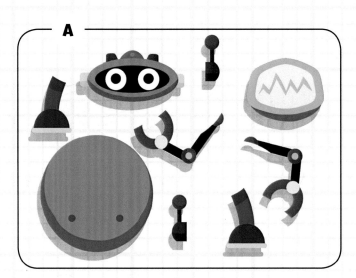

A

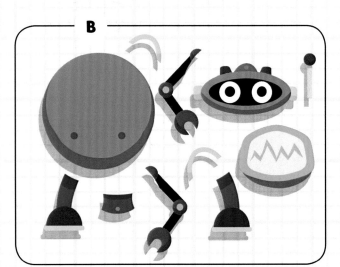

B

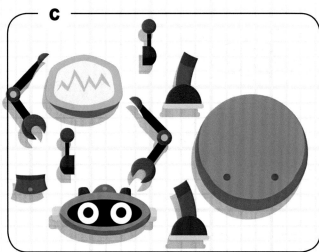

C

Crack Up

Which four pieces fit together to make the complete egg?

Mosaic Maker

Can you find the five groups of four squares in the mosaic?
None may be rotated.

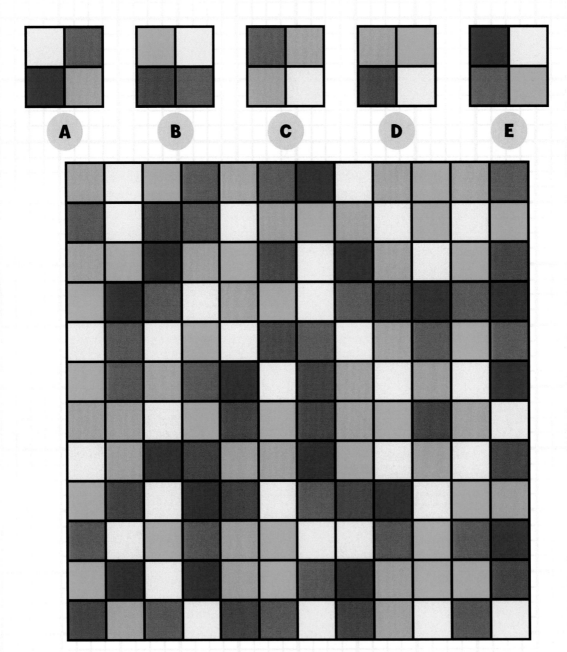

Gem Way

Find a way from the left side to the right side, moving on the gems in this order. You can move left, right, up, and down, but not diagonally.

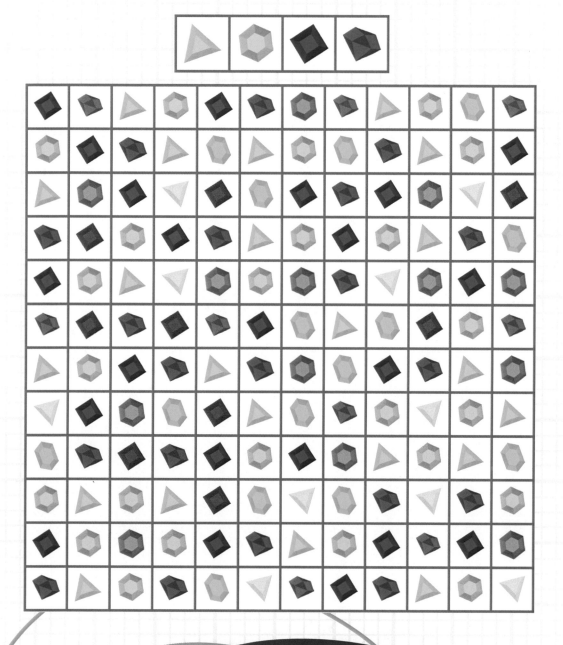

Chilly Changes

Spot 10 differences in the Arctic reflection.

Dragon Duos

Put the dragons into pairs that are exactly the same.
Some pairs face in opposite directions.

Bird Watch

Which bird is being described by each person?
They all chose a different bird.

My bird has a red-feathered head.

My bird cannot fly.

My bird has a long neck and long legs.

My bird has a curved beak.

My bird lives at the South Pole.

My bird has red, blue, and yellow feathers.

Cool Chameleons

Which silhouette exactly matches
this very rare chameleon?

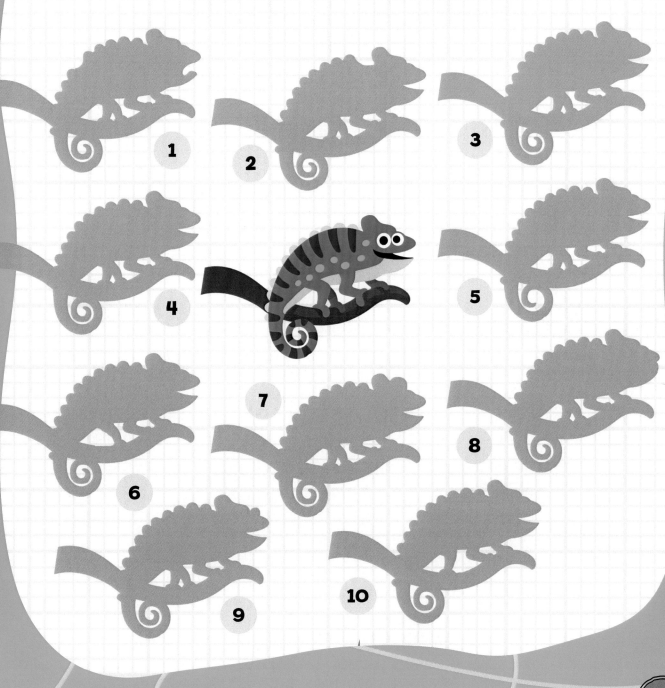

Pieces of the Past

Which set of pottery pieces will fit together to make this complete ancient vase?

Building Block

Which unfolded cube plan matches the finished building block?

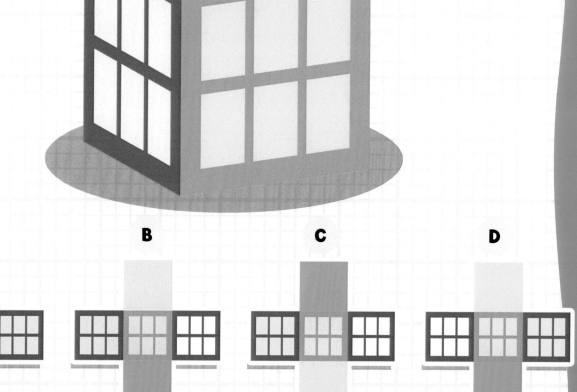

A   B   C   D

Island Way

At the "Start", follow each compass direction by that number of squares. N4 means you go north four squares, and so on. Where do you end up?

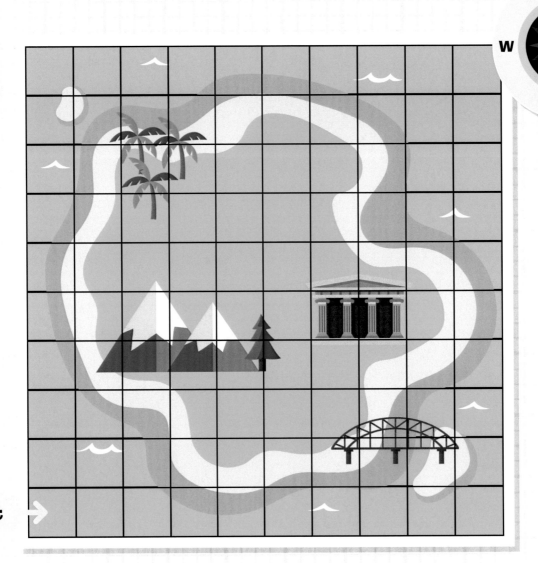

Start →

From the start, move N4, E7, N2, W1, N3, E2, S6, W4, N5, W2, S3, E4, S3, W3, N2, W3, and S4.

Toy Trouble

The twins both have exactly the same
toys, but one toy is missing from one set.
Figure out which one it is.

Bug Buddies

Can you find this group of four bug buddies?
The group is hiding in the larger group.

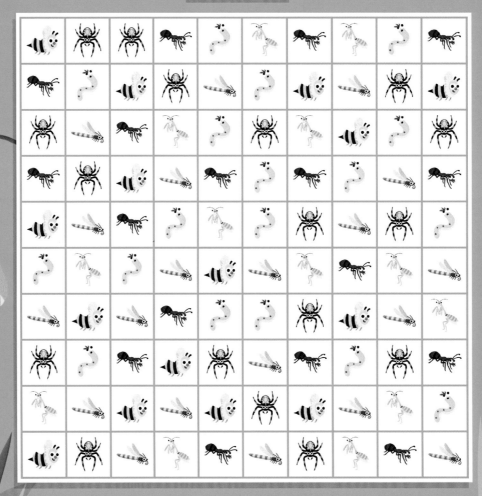

Star Baker

The baker's cupcakes have to be in perfect pairs. Find the six perfect pairs and the extra cupcake.

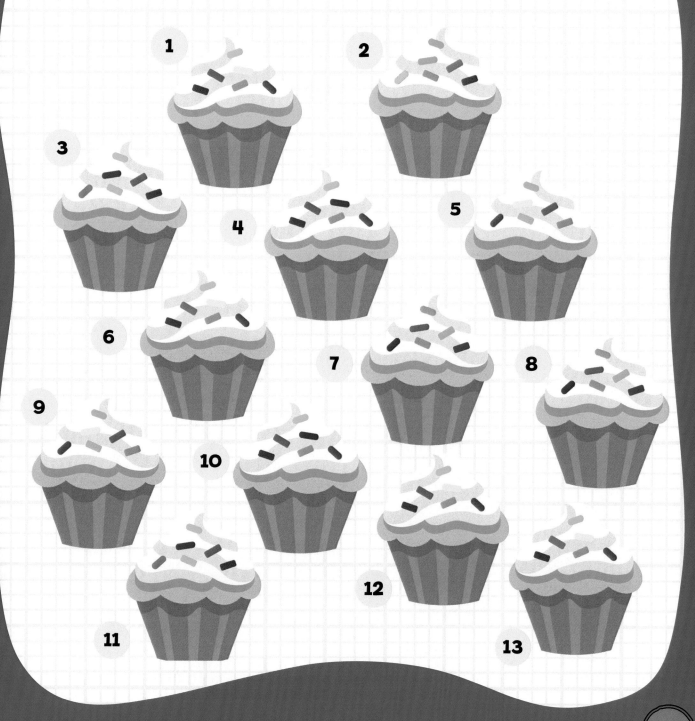

On the Leash

Follow the dogs' tangled leashes to discover their names.

1

2

3

4

5

Rex

Butch

Poppy

Digger

Maisy

Coral Clues

Can you spot the places in the coral reef where
the 8 circled close-ups appear?

1 2 3 4 5 6 7 8

Capture the King

Only one of these portraits perfectly depicts the king. Which one is it?

Beeing Different

Which bee is different from all the others?

Food Find

Can you find the foods with these outlines in the feast?

A

B

C

D

E

F

Home Port

The ship has arrived at the port. Using the directions it followed, can you discover where it sailed from? Hint: you will need to follow the directions in reverse.

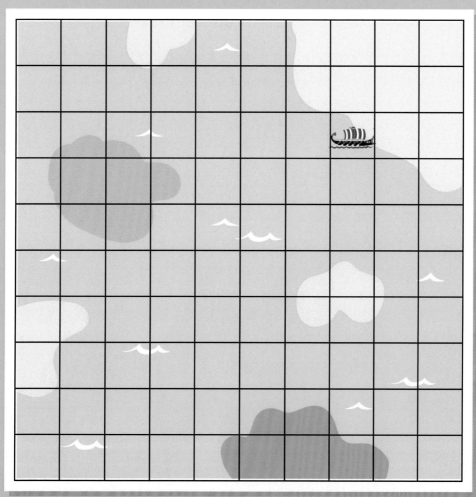

The ship sailed N3, W4, N2, W1, N3, E2, S1, E2.

Perfect Fit

Which group of shapes will fit together to make the large shape?

Answers

4. Rocket Route

5. Party Path

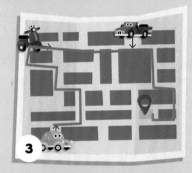

6. Hiker Trail

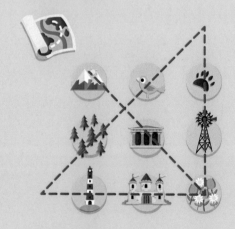

7. Bike Track

B

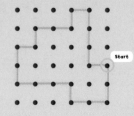

8. Robot Reboot

B

9. Crack Up

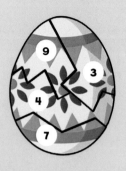

10. Mosaic Maker

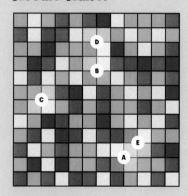

11. Gem Way

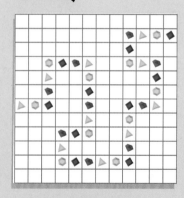

12. Chilly Challenges

29

13. Dragon Duos

14. Bird Watch
1 chose a woodpecker
2 chose an ostrich
3 chose a flamingo
4 chose an eagle
5 chose a penguin
6 chose a parrot

15. Cool Chameleons
3

16. Pieces of the Past
3

17. Building Block
B

18. Island Way
You end up back at the start!

19. Toy Trouble
The brick is missing from the set on the right.

20. Bug Buddies

21. Star Baker
1 and 12, 6 and 13,
4 and 10, 5 and 9,
7 and 8, 3 and 11
2 is the extra!

22. On the Leash
1. Digger, 2. Maisy, 3. Poppy
4. Rex, 5. Butch

23. Coral Clues

24. Capture the King
8

25. Beeing Different

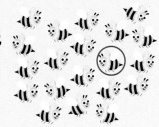

26. Food Find

27. Home Port

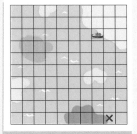

28. Perfect Fit
A

Glossary

coral reef A mass of coral just below the surface of the sea.

gems Jewels.

hive A structure in which bees are kept.

mosaic A design using small pieces of colored glass, pottery, or stone.

portraits Paintings, drawings, or photographs of people.

rotated Turned in a circular direction.

silhouette The solid, dark shape of something.

Further Information

Books

Brain Games for Clever Kids by Gareth Moore, Buster Books, 2014

Creative Picture Puzzles by Sarah Lawrence, Arcturus Publishing, 2017

The Best Puzzle Book Ever by Andy Peters, Arcturus Publishing, 2017

The Big Book of Kids' Puzzles by Jess Bradley, Arcturus Publishing, 2016

The Puzzle Activity Book, Buster Books, 2015

The Ultimate Puzzle Book by J. J. Wiggins, CreateSpace, 2016

Websites

https://www.bbc.co.uk/cbbc/joinin/bp-can-you-find-it-puzzles
Challenge your brain with these picture puzzles on the BBC website.

https://www.youtube.com/watch?v=8mJJrRRqYjs
Try this video of 28 picture puzzles and riddles.

Publisher's note to educators and parents: Our editors have carefully reviewed these websites to ensure that they are suitable for students. Many websites change frequently, however, and we cannot guarantee that a site's future contents will continue to meet our high standards of quality and educational value. Be advised that students should be closely supervised whenever they access the internet.

Index

Published in 2020 by Windmill Books,
an Imprint of Rosen Publishing
29 East 21st Street, New York, NY 10010

Copyright © Arcturus Holdings Ltd, 2020

All rights reserved. No part of this book may be
reproduced in any form without permission in
writing from the publisher, except by a reviewer.

Edited by Kate Overy and Joe Harris
Written by Kate Overy
Illustrated by Ed Myer and Graham Rich
Designed by Trudi Webb and Emma Randall

Cataloging-in-Publication Data

Names: Regan, Lisa.
Title: Amazing observation puzzles / Lisa Regan.
Description: New York : Windmill Books, 2020. |
Series: Brain blasters | Includes glossary and index.
Identifiers: ISBN 9781725394339 (pbk.) |
ISBN 9781725394353 (library bound) | ISBN
9781725394346 (6 pack)
Subjects: LCSH: Puzzles–Juvenile literature. | Logic
puzzles–Juvenile literature. | Picture puzzles–Juvenile
literature.
Classification: LCC GV1493.R465 2020 |
DDC 793.8–dc23

Manufactured in the United States of America

CPSIA Compliance Information: Batch BW20WM: For Further Information
contact Rosen Publishing, New York, New York at 1-800-237-9932